ꓕURN SHⱯKE ꓞLIP

Creative Director **Danielle DeVoe**
Editors **Caitlin Fitzgerald and Alexandra Rowley**
Managing Editor **Robert Goff**
Project Manager **Linda Fiske**
Foreword by **Mireille Guiliano**
Essay by **Stephen Wallis**

The editors would like to thank all
of the participating artists and also
Chelsea Hadley
Michael Hall
Judith Nesbitt
Gail Brodie
Michael Hue-Williams
Elizabeth Kane
Heather Williams

Cover images top to bottom:
Andrew French, *La Grande Dame*, 2001, gelatin silver print
John Dugdale, *Christ Our Liberator, Morton Street, NYC*, 1999, Cyanotype print
Susan Derges, *The Observer & The Observed #5*, 1990, gelatin silver print

Designed by P²+M, Inc., New York

This book is printed on 170 gsm. Lumi-Silk Matte art paper
The typefaces used in this book are Minion, NeuzeitS and ScalaSans

Printed and bound in China

ISBN: 0-9712978-0-0

⊥URN SH∆KE ⅎLIP

www.eyestorm.com

In the early 1800s, the House of Veuve Clicquot transformed the art of creating fine Champagne with three simple gestures: a turn, a shake and a flip. Each motion, direct and powerful, helped turn the dream of crystal clear Champagne—as envisioned by one young remarkable woman—into reality.

Madame "Veuve" Clicquot (1777-1866) discovered that turning, shaking and flipping individual bottles of bubbly over time would render Champagne truly clear and sparkling for the first time in history. This clarifying technique, which collects the wine's sediment in the bottle's neck from which it can be expelled, is known as "riddling" or "*remuage.*" It revolutionized the *méthode champenoise*.

Madame Clicquot's creativity influenced the world of wine in a literal way. In a more abstract fashion, fine art has the ability to change the way we view the world. Art has the power to turn ideas around, shake up the status quo, and even invite its audience to "flip" over a new way of seeing.

Art, like wine, has the ability to transform the spirit. From the first glance at an image or a label, fine art and fine wine set up expectations. The successful work of art exceeds those expectations in the person experiencing it, whether through the medium photography, drawing or Champagne. Making Champagne is indeed an art. It takes a precise combination of grapes, soil, location and climate, and the very human artistry of assembling still wines from many vineyards in the Champagne region, and sometimes several vintages, into a unique blend that is aged for years before being released. Cellarmasters are artists more than alchemists or scientists, though they are a little of all three. For me, as for many, Champagne is the most evocative wine. The pop of the cork lightens the spirit and promises celebration. In each bottle there is a special message and rich experience. The aromas, flavors and associations found in a glass can transport us to another place, even another time. For the art lover, colors, shapes and space ignite similar journeys. A great work of art transforms the commonplace.

In this collaboration with eyestorm, some of the world's most compelling and rewarding contemporary artists and photographers showcase their work. We're honored to have them associated with "*La Grande Dame de la Champagne,*" the "great lady" who transformed the Champagne maker's art. And we're proud that for over two hundred years, artists from around the world have celebrated some of life's greatest moments with the Champagnes of Madame Clicquot.

"If one is lucky, a solitary fantasy can totally transform one million realities," the poet Maya Angelou wrote. That is the gift and promise of art, whether on the printed page, in a painting, or poured into a delicate flute. To define the allure of the images in *Turn, Shake, Flip* is akin to describing the world's finest wines—elusive until experienced.

Enjoy the exploration.

Mireille Guiliano
President & CEO, Clicquot, Inc.
Director, Champagne Veuve Clicquot

Veuve Clicquot
LA GRANDE DAME
Champagne

We live in a golden age for photography.

After a century and a half of debate, scholars, museums and collectors now embrace photography as the unequivocal peer of painting and sculpture. This is true particularly for younger generations, from Baby Boomers to today's youths, whose culture is defined by an ever-increasing barrage of images from films, television, advertising and the Internet. Photography is the foundation of our everyday visual language, and we accept its place in art as a matter of course.

Walk into galleries from London to New York to Tokyo, and you'll find them filled with photographic works, many aspiring to the scale and visual impact of a Jackson Pollock or a panoramic 19th-century landscape. Large-format, intensely hued images, whose dimensions are measured in feet rather than inches, are ascendant in the age of Imax. Artists such as Andreas Gursky and Thomas Struth create giant, vividly detailed photographic tableaux that document—even fetishize—the places of commerce and culture, the domestic spaces and the rituals that define contemporary society.

New digital technologies have radically altered contemporary art, allowing artists to manipulate photographic images by adding or removing elements, altering colors, transforming the supposedly objective image into a created one. For those who look to photographs for objective truth, this is perhaps disconcerting news. But for artists, the ability to manipulate photographs has thrown the door wide open to a world of unprecedented creative possibilities—and new realities. As Flaubert put it, "Everything you invent is true."

The range of photo-based art being made is staggering, and no single book on the subject could hope to be truly comprehensive. The selection of images presented here by eyestorm and Veuve Clicquot, curated by Caitlin Fitzgerald and Alexandra Rowley, offers an engaging cross-section of contemporary art photography, a testament to the diversity of photography as an artistic medium. The artists include some who are exclusively photographers and some who work primarily in other mediums; some who are famous and whose work sells for tens of thousands of dollars, and some who work in relative obscurity. But they are all immensely talented and their work reflects the history, scope and promise of photo-based art.

Investigating Reality

A dominant characteristic of art photography today is the desire to challenge notions of reality and truth in pictures. Photography's illusory nature is the stock-in-trade of Vik Muniz, a master at creating such visual sleights of hand as pictures of cotton that mimic Alfred Stieglitz's famous cloud studies or reproductions of landscapes by Constable and Corot that he made using thread. His 1994 photograph *Fiat Lux (Lightbulb)* (plate 09), from the series *Pictures of Wire*, appears to be a drawing of a lightbulb. In fact, it is a photograph of a wire sculpture of a bulb, meticulously handmade by the artist.

Laura Carton's photograph of a hotel bed, *Untitled #7*, 2000 (plate 08), looks like a view of a chambermaid's work-in-progress. The sheets are pulled off and the split mattress is separated down the middle. But the room is actually the setting of a pornographic photo, taken from the Internet and digitally stripped of its actors. There is no sign of the steamy activity that was once the image's subject—not even a dimple on the mattress created by an elbow or knee—and we are left completely to our own imaginations to fill in what's missing. Which is more banal, Carton seems to be asking, an empty hotel room or a still of an X-rated romp? How does knowing about the erased porn scene affect our sense of reality and the multitude of erased scenes we walk through, pass over, and sleep on every day?

Whether using digital manipulation or strictly conventional means, artists today are making photographs of sometimes elaborately staged fictions. Among the best-known artists working in this vein are Cindy Sherman, Jeff Wall, Gregory Crewdson and Peter Garfield. Strongly influenced by movies, Garfield's *Mobile Home (Safe)*, 1997 (plate 29), makes obvious reference to the *Wizard of Oz* with its house sailing through the air. The image, which is not computer generated or manipulated, evokes a Cheeveresque undercurrent of the bizarre that runs through suburban America.

Such images are often just "real" enough to make you pause, but you're not likely to mistake them for reality. Sometimes, the artificiality is part of the intended aesthetic. It's an approach that is used in contemporary fashion photography, much of which has become deliberately mannered, self-consciously ironic and self-referential. The high-keyed work of David LaChapelle delivers campy spectacle that may not be everyone's taste—but its impact is unforgettable. Images such as his *Madonna: West Side Highway, New York* (plate 34), offer a vision of pop culture that is ultra-vivid, more real than reality.

Art and fashion have grown ever closer in recent decades, nowhere more so than in contemporary art photography. Wolfgang Tillmans has had a foot in both worlds, as his images of youth culture from the early '90s were an important influence on ad campaigns of top fashion houses. A far cry from LaChapelle's stagy fantasies, Tillmans' work is more direct, more human and more intimate, typified by his 1996 image *Faltenwurf (Boxed)* (plate 15), a simple composition of clothes crumpled in a box. The items of clothing, stripped of a marketing glaze, become aesthetic objects and, as with much of Tillmans' work, seem to subvert fashion's conventional ideals of glamour, sophistication and perfection.

Symbolic Gestures

One of art's most prominent veterans represented in this collection of images—along with Ed Ruscha, Dennis Oppenheim and William Wegman—is Ralph Gibson. His *Untitled* (plate 03) comes from his recent *Ex Libris* series, featuring high-contrast black-and-white images of historical books, manuscripts and other objects that serve as rich symbols of the history of human language and knowledge.

Using symbols of a more personal nature, Marianne Courville creates haunting photographs from old home movies. Her image of a female diver under water (plate 20) is part of her 1997 series *Based on a True Story*. Inspired by the loss of childhood memories after her father's sudden death, Courville reexamined Super 8 films shot by her father and grandfather decades ago, and then made Ilfochrome prints of stills from those films. The results represent the process of her recovering lost memories and understanding her family's past. These deeply personal images of self-exploration achieve an uncommon and subtle elegance that is rare in our age of treacly confessionals and cheap talk-show therapy.

Two very different photographs by Arne Svenson present symbols of psychological despair. The first, from his 1994 *Suicide* series, is a searing image of a single strand of rope, suspended in a blank space (plate 07). Tightly coiled and frayed, the rope is a powerful evocation of a psyche come undone. The second image, more ambiguous, is a view of the Excalibur casino in Las Vegas, taken in 1999 (plate 13). The casino, with its Disneyesque, castellated exterior, appears distant and impenetrable; the view from the empty parking lot seems desperate, that of someone in dire need of a break. Does the yellow arrow painted on the asphalt in the foreground warn the viewer away from temptation? Or is it a hopeful sign that luck will turn?

Art in the Everyday

Striking a different tone are more felicitous vignettes such as Serge J.F. Levy's 1998 photograph of a boy doing a back flip on the beach at Coney Island (plate 55) or Lisa Kereszi's image of whirling dervishes at the Cathedral of St. John the Divine, from 1996 (plate 24). Other works reveal the poetry in ordinary objects, including Susan Lipper's picture of salt and sugar shakers on a spotted tablecloth (plate 38), one of a series of photographs of everyday life that Lipper took between 1993 and 1998 while traveling across the U.S.

The quotidian also rings transcendent in Donald Sultan's exquisite photographs of smoke (plates 22-23). These images, which served as the basis for a series of Sultan's paintings, capture the beauty and the infinite variations in the rings and vortices of smoke emanating from the artist's cigar.

There are several images in this selection of photographs that capture the lyricism and wonder of the natural world, including Robert Vizzini's *Inside Looking Out* (plate 04), an extended exposure of the nighttime sky taken in Chianti, Italy, in 1999, which records the movement of the stars. Taking a more terrestrial subject, Frederic Ohringer's still life of a cabbage heart, from 1991 (plate 11), is not only formally exquisite but also vaguely anthropomorphic. Ohringer's image calls to mind Edward Weston's well-known studies of peppers and nautilus shells and evokes a long tradition of still life photography.

The Beauty of Process

The traditions and history of photography have prompted some artists to look backward and explore photographic processes from the past. In this age of digital images and point-and-shoot cameras, there is rich territory to be mined in the time-consuming and often labor-intensive old ways of making pictures. Some examples here include Jerry Spagnoli's untitled daguerreotype of Times Square, from 2000 (plate 65); Dan Estabrook's salt print *Untitled (Melancholia)*, from 1995 (plate 51); and Abelardo Morell's 1999 *Camera Obscura Image of the Chrysler Building in Hotel Room* (plate 48). For her 1997 photogram *River Taw* (plate 42), Susan Derges placed light-sensitive paper in a stream at night and fired a flash gun to capture the subtle but dazzling surface textures of the water. In works such as these, the process is central to the work's ultimate meaning.

James Welling's *1A* (plate 41), from 1998, started with a photogram, which he made by placing strips of paper on a photosensitive sheet and exposing it to light. He then digitally scanned the photogram and made high-contrast negatives of that image. The final prints were made from these negatives. In the finished prints, what had been bands of white on the photogram were now black, resulting in a dynamic image that seems to reference, among other things, the bold slashes of the Abstract Expressionist painter Franz Kline.

Coming Full Circle

In choosing the images for this book, the theme *Turn, Shake, Flip* has not so much been applied literally as it has served as a starting point. It might be obvious why Amy Steiner's *Untitled (Eve in Boat)*, 1998 (plate 01), a photograph of a young woman at the rear of a wooden sailboat turning her head, is in the *Turn* section, but unless you recognize the poles on the stage in Lisa Kereszi's *Steps to the Stage, Strip Club, New Orleans, LA*, 2001 (plate 35), you'll probably have to read the title to understand why it's in the *Shake* section. All of the images were selected for their visual and conceptual strength, and the results speak powerfully for themselves.

The photograph—along with the printing press, the personal computer, and the Internet—is among the most significant inventions of the past 500 years. It is a tool for documentation, communication and, of course, aesthetic creation, capable of an almost infinite variety of expression. In these early days of the 21st century, photography is arguably the dominant artistic medium—greater and more pervasive than painting, sculpture, even music or film. In April 1839, the *New Yorker* published an article announcing the development of the daguerreotype, the first widely used process for making photographs. In the piece the author prophesized, "Here, in truth, is a discovery launched upon the world, that must make a revolution in art." More than 160 years later, that revolution continues.

Stephen Wallis
Executive Editor, *Art & Auction* magazine

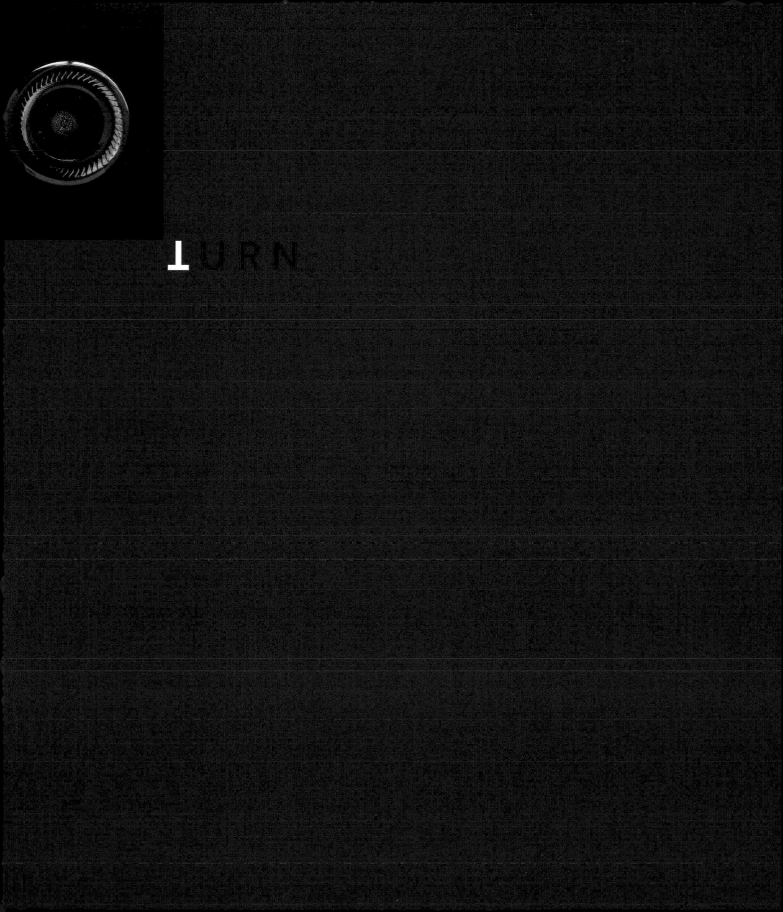

TURN

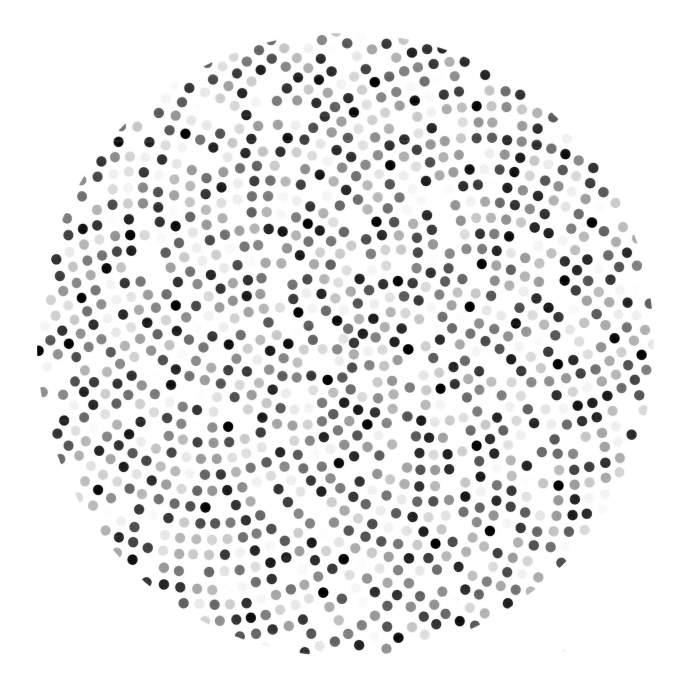

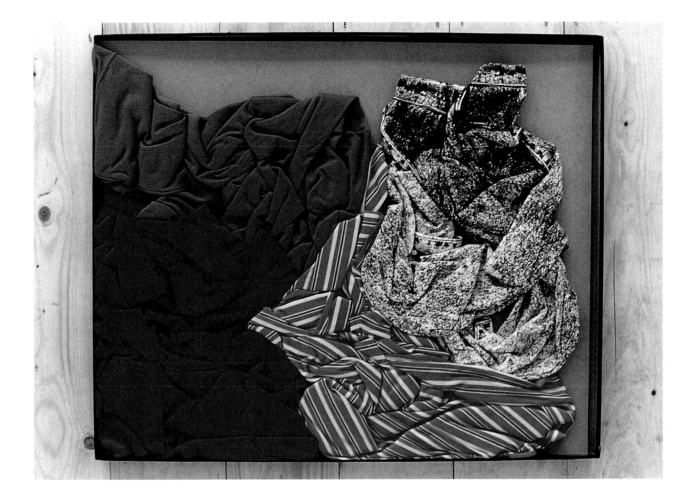

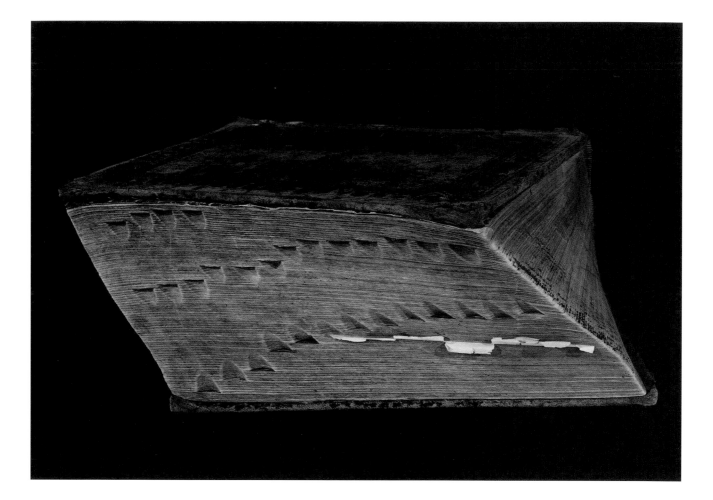

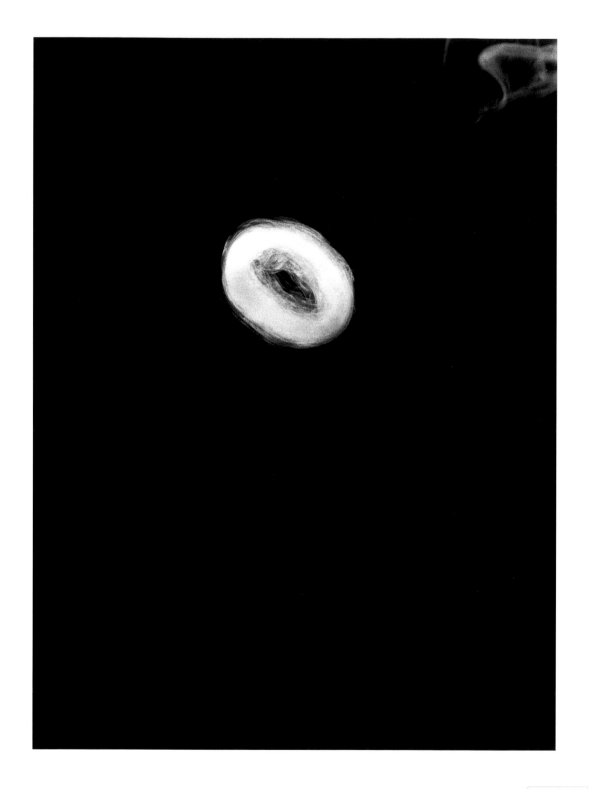

SH△KE

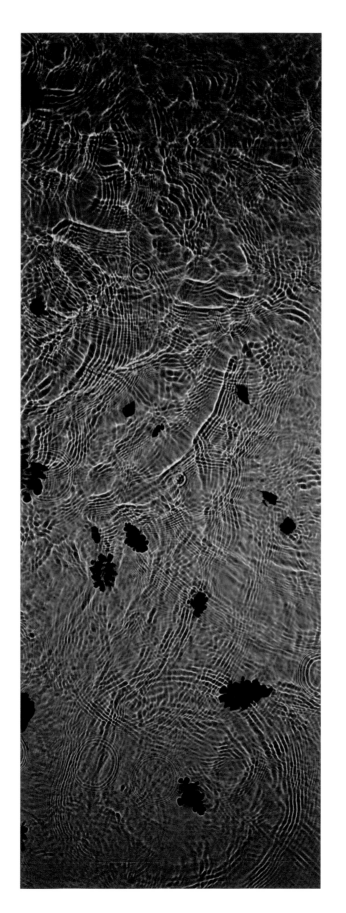

FLIP

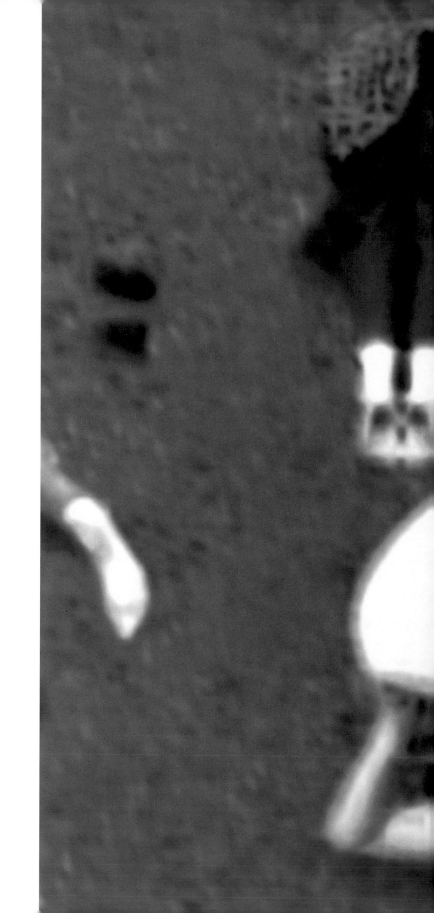

Spontaneous position of
catatonic melancholia

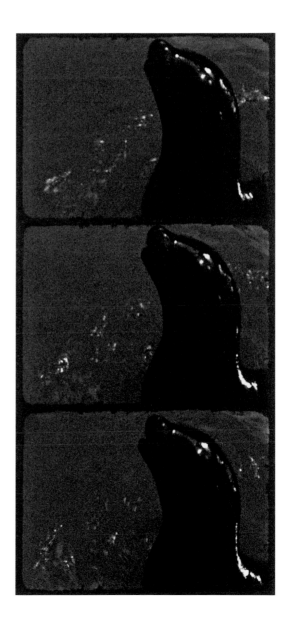

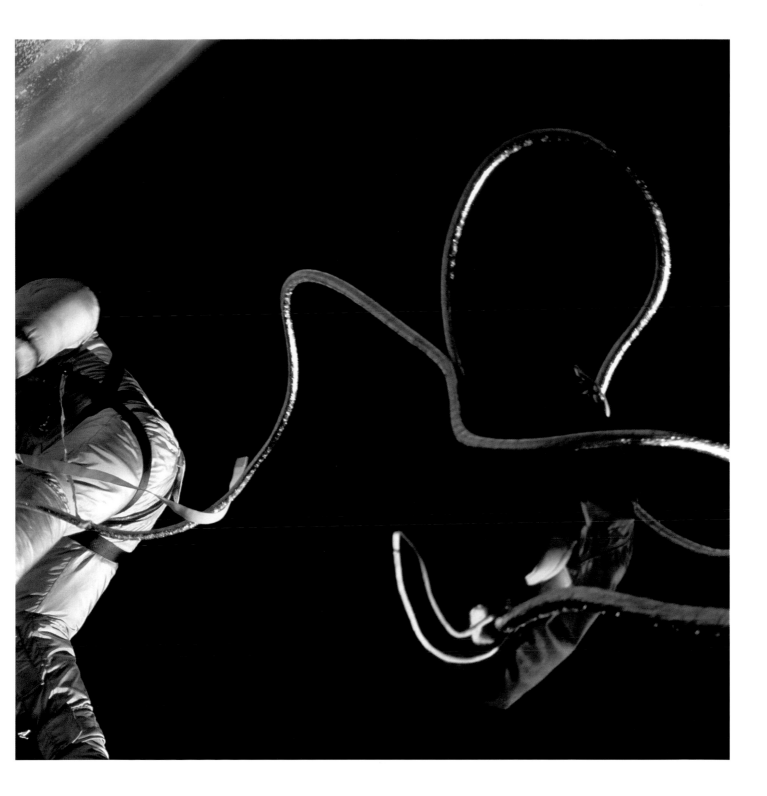

TURN

01. **Amy Steiner**
Untitled (Eve in Boat), 1998
Ilfochrome print
Courtesy of Rare Art Properties, NY

02. **Peter Lindbergh**
Lynn Koester, Comme des Garçons, Paris, 1984
gelatin silver print
Courtesy of the artist

03. **Ralph Gibson**
Untitled, from the *Ex Libris* series, 1983
gelatin silver print
Courtesy of the artist

04. **Robert Vizzini**
Inside Looking Out, 1999
silver lith print
Courtesy of the artist and ClampArt, NY

05. **Sol LeWitt**
Bands of Equal Width in Color, 2000
linocut on paper
Courtesy of the artist

06. **William Wegman**
Looking Back, 2001
Iris print
Courtesy of the artist

07. **Arne Svenson**
Rope, from the *Suicide* series, 1994
gelatin silver print
Courtesy of the artist and Julie Saul Gallery

08. **Laura Carton**
Untitled #7, 2000
digital c-print
Courtesy of the artist

09. **Vik Muniz**
Fiat Lux (lightbulb), from the *Pictures of Wire* series, 1994
gelatin silver print
Courtesy of the artist

10. **Damien Hirst**
Valium, 2000
Lambda print
Courtesy of the artist and eyestorm

11. **Frederic Ohringer**
Cabbage Heart, 1991
gelatin silver print
Courtesy of the artist

12. **Ed Ruscha**
Street Meets Avenue, 2000
lithograph
Courtesy of the artist

13. **Arne Svenson**
Las Vegas: New York NY Reflected in the Excalibur Hotel, 1999
c-print
Courtesy of the artist and Julie Saul Gallery, NY

14. **Andrew Zuckerman**
Turnpike, New Jersey, 2000
color print
Courtesy of the artist

15. **Wolfgang Tillmans**
Faltenwurf (boxed), 1996
c-print
Courtesy of the artist and Andrea Rosen Gallery, NY

16. **Fawn Potash**
Big Dictionary #1, 1995
toned gelatin silver print with wax
Courtesy of the artist and Gallery 292, NY

17. **Mike & Doug Starn**
Black Pulse #11, 2000-2001
Lambda Fuji-Flex print
Courtesy of the artist

18. **Debra Vilen**
Snow Wolf, 2001
pigment print
Courtesy of the artist

19. **Dennis Oppenheim**
Whirlpool, 1973
Iris print
Courtesy of the artist and eyestorm

20. **Marianne Courville**
Untitled (Blue Lady), 1970/1997
Ilfochrome print
Courtesy of the artist

21. **James Whitlow Delano**
Staircase in St. Isaacs Cathedral, St. Petersburg, Russia, 1999
gelatin silver print
Courtesy of the artist

22. **Donald Sultan**
Smoke Rings XV, 1997
gelatin silver print
Courtesy of the artist

23. **Donald Sultan**
Smoke Rings XXV, 1997
gelatin silver print
Courtesy of the artist

24. **Lisa Kereszi**
Whirling Dervishes at St. John the Divine, NYC, 1996
c-print
Courtesy of the artist

SHAKE

25. **Jessica Wynne**
Untitled, 1997
c-print
Courtesy of the artist

26. **Charles Richardson**
Mr. Palomar Takes to the Street, 1999
selenium-toned silver gelatin print
Courtesy of the artist

27. **John Dugdale**
Christ Our Liberator, Morton Street, NYC, 1999
Cyanotype print
Courtesy of the artist

28. **Douglas Dubler**
Tiffany Glass #292, 2001
archival digital pigment print,
Courtesy of the artist

29. **Peter Garfield**
Mobile Home (Safe), 1997
c-print
Courtesy of the artist and Feigen
Contemporary, NY

30. **Bettina Witteveen**
Medusae 3 of 3, from the
Transformation series, 1999
color photograph
Courtesy of the artist

31. **Lorraine DePietro**
Conversation, 2001
gelatin silver print
Courtesy of the artist

32. **Heidi Siedlecki**
Corridor #1, 1995
gelatin silver print
Courtesy of the artist

33. **James Whitlow Delano**
Dogon Dancers, Begnmento, Mali, 1998
gelatin silver print
Courtesy of the artist

34. **David LaChapelle**
Madonna: West Side Highway, New York, 1998
color photograph
Courtesy of David LaChapelle Studio

35. **Lisa Kereszi**
Steps to the Stage, Strip Club, New Orleans, LA, 2001
c-print
Courtesy of the artist

36. **Blair Rainey**
Evacuation, 1992
digital c-print
(Original from super 8mm filmstrips)
Courtesy of the artist

37. **Suzette Bross**
Roller Coaster #1, 2001
digital print
Courtesy of the artist

38. **Susan Lipper**
Untitled, from the *trip* series, 1993-1998
gelatin silver print
Courtesy of the artist

39. **Andrew French**
Fatima, 2001
toned gelatin silver print
Courtesy of the artist

40. **Andrew Zuckerman**
Galapagos, 2000
color photograph
Courtesy of the artist

41. **James Welling**
1A, 1998
gelatin silver print
Courtesy of the artist and Gorney,
Bravin & Lee, NY

42. **Susan Derges**
River Taw, 1997
Ilfochrome print
Courtesy of the artist and eyestorm

FLIP

43. **Stuart Hawkins**
Tumblers, 1999
c-print
Courtesy of the artist

44. **Susan Lipper**
Untitled, from the *trip* series, 1993-1998
gelatin silver print
Courtesy of the artist

45. **Ralph Gibson**
Sandra, Los Angeles, 1963
gelatin silver print
Courtesy of the artist

46. **Ari Marcopolous**
Rippey, Tignes, 1998
gelatin silver print
Courtesy of the artist

47. **Howard Schatz**
Balance, 1998
gelatin silver print
Courtesy of the artist and SoHo Triad Fine Arts, NY

48. **Abelardo Morell**
Camera Obscura Image of the Chrysler Building in Hotel Room, 1999
gelatin silver print
Courtesy Bonni Benrubi Gallery, NY

49. **Kara Cressman**
Tarot Color Portrait (Lara), 2001
c-print
Courtesy of the artist

50. **Katalin Kotvics**
Ascent, 1998
gelatin silver print
Courtesy of the artist

51. **Dan Estabrook**
Untitled (Melancholia), 1995
salt print with ink
Courtesy of the artist and Sarah Morthland Gallery, NY

52. **Vera Lutter**
Zeppelin Friedrichshafen I:
August 10-13, 1999
unique gelatin silver print
Courtesy of the artist and Fraenkel Gallery, SF

53. **Marianne Courville**
Untitled, from the *Otton Lazar* series,
2000/2001
Roland Hi-Fi inkjet print
Courtesy of the artist

54. **Susan Derges**
The Observer & The Observed #5, 1990
gelatin silver print
Courtesy of the artist and eyestorm

55. **Serge J. F. Levy**
Boy Playing Hooky, from the
Coney Island series, 1998
gelatin silver print
Courtesy of the artist

56. **Michael Light**
Full Moon #12 from the project
Full Moon, 1999
direct digital c-print
Courtesy of the artist

57. **Roe Etheridge**
Window with Bahama Blinds, 1997
c-print
Courtesy of the artist

58. **Carol Cohen**
Goose Air, Brooklyn, 2000
Kodachrome
Courtesy of the artist

59. **Mark Cohen**
Untitled
(up side down girl), 1974
gelatin silver print
Courtesy of the artist and
Bruce Silverstein Gallery, NY

60. **Sandra Nydegger**
Cowtown, NJ, from the *East Coast*
Rodeo Circuit series, 1999
gelatin silver print
Courtesy of the artist

61. **Ari Marcopolous**
Terje, Laguna Beach, 1997
gelatin silver print
Courtesy of the artist

62. **Jessica Wynne**
Untitled, 2000
c-print
Courtesy of the artist

63. **Martin Kersels**
Still from "Pink Constellation", 2001
DVD
Courtesy of the artist and Deitch Projects, NY

64. **Alvin Booth**
Untitled #950869, 1995
uniquely toned gelatin silver print
Courtesy of the artist and Yancey
Richardson Gallery, NY

65. **Jerry Spagnoli**
Untitled, 2000
Daguerreotype
Courtesy of the artist

66. **Ralph Gibson**
Self-Portrait, Los Angeles, 1969
gelatin silver print
Courtesy of the artist

TURN

Andrew French
La Grande Dame, 2001
gelatin silver print
Courtesy of Champagne Veuve Clicquot

SHAKE

Andrew French
Riddler's Hand, 2001
gelatin silver print
Courtesy of Champagne Veuve Clicquot

FLIP

Laurent Gorget
Aging in the Cellars, 2000
gelatin silver print
Courtesy of Champagne Veuve Clicquot